Words with nowhere to go

Madison North

 BookLeaf Publishing

Presentation by *BookLeaf Publishing*

Web: www.bookleafpub.com

E-mail: info@bookleafpub.com

ISBN: 9789357696685

First edition 2022

DEDICATION

To my sweet girl

You are limitless.

Always be authentically you.

Intense

You look at me
with such seriousness
I've never felt before.
And I have felt enough
from more than a few.
You demand the attention
of those around you.
I forget to over think
because I am now invulnerable.
And although
your eyes are so dark,
just several shades brighter than black,
they are my new
favourite
colour.

Karma.

As you're rocking
back and forth,
into her.
Like a boat tied to the shore
in a violent storm.
I hope you see me
as you come
— undone.

Absent

My head in the c l o u d s.
And yours,
between my legs.

Come back to me baby.

Palliative

I know you're done with life,
relentless in every way.
The only thing we can do now,
is close our eyes and pray.

I'm sorry I can't do more.

T

G

This

Staring at your chubby face,
your eyes start to softly close.
Long lashes fan against your cheeks.
A tiny button nose.

You look up at me and smile.
Snuggling into my chest even more.
I rock you back to sleep again,
but in no way, is this a chore.

As one day you wont need me,
to hold you while you drift.
You'll be more independent.
So I see this as a gift.

To hold you close,
and breathe you in.
I'll memorise it all.
The softness of your skin.
This, I will recall.

-motherhood

Side note:

People are no more
and will never be more
than just people
— so live your life for you

BE . BETTER

I cry for your children
because they
deserve
Better

More than life

How kind and loving and sweet you are. The love
you have bought into my life is indescribable but I
am feeling it right now and I can't stop crying.
Not of sadness, but pure gratitude.
You are my biggest success in life and I can not thank
your soul enough, for choosing me to be your mum
and giving me this opportunity of growth to be better
for you.
I love you more than life.

Not today

It's hard to have others
in my home
when I feel everything
as my own.

-empath

Control

One day you'll wake up,
but in a completely different way.

You'll come to realise,
you've been in control the whole time.

You'll take responsibility
for your part in your suffering.

And you'll heal
And you'll grow
And you'll finally come alive

Wake up

I feel as if I'm not good enough.
Scared to share my voice.
But recently it's dawned on me,
I do not have a choice.

My words get all jumbled
When I try to speak.
I doubt myself and worry,
they may think that I'm a freak.

But then, I am reminded,
at the very end of the day.
I am proud of who I am,
so I'll say it anyway!

Why should I keep quiet,
shut up and not be heard.
I am strong and fierce and free.
FREE. Just like a bird.

So I'll share my thoughts and feelings,
on this corruption we all call life.
You have absolutely No idea,
how the world is in such strife.

Planet earth is utterly fucked.
Something NEEDS to change.
Violence, hate, denial. What?
You don't think it's a little strange?

We blindly follow orders,
don't think to question why.
Wake up! You've been conditioned!
Been fed lie after lie.

Take this as your wake up call,
to decondition your mind.
Just, please don't turn the other way,
and act as if you're blind.

Different

You are different, this feels right.
Kind and gentle, love and light.

I feel it already,
in the depth of my soul.
You're the one that I want.
You make me feel whole.

So please don't you leave me,
in the middle of the night.
Because you are different,
And this feels right.

Flow

Life is not meant,
to stay the same.
Could you imagine?
It would be so lame.

So embrace the change,
Go with the flow.
The ups and downs,
The high, the low.

Sunshine

She had a warmth about her, no matter the day
you had, her warmth would spread over you and
you would feel comforted and relaxed.
Like a hot drink on a cold rainy day.

-my Nan

T

T

T

www.ingramcontent.com/pod-product-compliance
Lightning Source LLC
LaVergne TN
LVHW051249200726
843510LV00011B/1755